Writings fro

Written by
Estella Wells

(aka The Poetess)

CONTENTS

Foreword

I first met Estella Isaac Wells when we were juniors in college enrolled in the same literature class, a class in which we not only studied the work of well-known writers, we wrote poetry of our own. It seems especially fitting that years later, never mind how many, I'm presented with the opportunity to offer a foreword for her poetry collection. Beyond the cosmic symmetry of it, however, it is also an honor and my pleasure.

Estella's poetry is enlivened by the same energy and spirit that characterizes her as a person: a genuine warmth and exuberant engagement with the world and the people in it, along with a keen mind and a deep and abiding faith. You'll find all of those qualities in the poems in this collection.

Poetry is both art and craft, inspired, evocative language distilling human experience in a way that stirs human emotion, allowing readers to see life, the world, and oftentimes themselves and others in new ways. As a poet, Estella allows herself to be inspired by life, and that inspiration moves her pen, allowing her to capture what is truest.

I believe readers will find the poetry that flows from her pen, her truth, profoundly moving.

Indeed, in tone and timbre, I would put much of Estella's work in conversation with such poems as Maya Angelou's "Phenomenal Woman" and "Still I Rise," her poems sharing the latter's resolute sense of promise and pride.

The poems themselves, the keen vision, the heartfelt emotion, and the clear love of the written word are Estella's own, and the energy that pulses through this poetry beats in time with her own heart.

As you read these poems, you'll no doubt feel the thrumming heartbeat of them, as you find yourself enlivened and inspired by the energy, the language, and the vision of the poet, my friend, Estella Isaac Wells.

Dr. Yolanda Manora
Associate Professor

One Word

How did you know the way to wake me up
All tingly and excited?
A word
Just one
One that will make me guess its meaning,
One that will make me search and find
A word that will puzzle the "around the way girl" But will
entice the one who's a little bad and bougie

One word
Catering to my intellect
Damn, boy! You're talkin' sexy to me
Intelligentsia
Insouciant
Equally pleasing
In Spanish or French

To the English major in me
That one word is manna from heaven
It's almost as intoxicating
As the sweet, smooth taste of Moscato

It tickles my palate
And gives me a heady rush

One word

Giddy

Definitions: "To be joyfully elated. Euphoric."
"Having a sensation of whirling and a tendency to fall or
stagger."
My heart races at the sight of you
How can I be nervous and confident at the same time?
Like a schoolgirl
Like riding a roller coaster
That orgasmic-like feeling
When you can almost reach the sky,
Then feel the rush of coming down
Feelings of breathlessness
Anticipation
Do you ever have a conversation with yourself? When you're
in the early stages of dating?

Me 1: Okay, I might not be perfect, but I know there are
people who would love to be my size.

Me 2: Girl, you look good. Keep looking at those YouTube
videos so you can get that sexy dance down.

Me 1: Oh no! Am I like one of those Facebook posts? "How you think you look vs. How you really look."

Me 2: Girl, you good.

Me 1: Does he really like me? Is Steve Harvey right? They know early on whether it's a "Bring her home to Mom / potential wifey" thing or a "This is what grown folks do, we're just kickin' it" thing.
Is it an "I like you, but not like that!" thing?

Me 2: Calm down!

Me 1: Okay. I'm going to reread his texts and try to read the subliminal messages.
What he said, but what is he REALLY saying?

Me 2: Girl, he likes you. Remember who you are and whose you are. Radiate the light from within.

Me 1: Calling on my Yahyah sisters.
Nam-myoho-renge-kyo.
Inhale peace. Exhale confusion.
Iyanla, Susan, Oprah, Johnetta B. Cole, Angela B.
My pulse has now slowed to its regular pace …
Then I think of him …
And I'm giddy.

On Your 29th

Birthday girl, so bright and so fair
What can I say on this special day?
Ok, that's a little cheesy, so let me start again

Because tomorrow is never promised,
I want you to always remember
That you are loved
That you are making an amazing impact, and
That you are a phenomenally phenomenal woman

Called by different names:
Isaac, Jasmine, Jazzy, Sis, Baby Girl, Mija
Birmingham-born (she likes grits)
Cali-raised (tacos, enchiladas y burritos)
This boho-chic woman now calls Washington home

Arms outstretched, giving hugs to strangers
Fiercely independent and determined
From "I can do it by myself" as a little girl,
To driving across the country solo as an adult

Always remember, never forget
That you are loved and admired
You are a phenomenally phenomenal woman

Third-generation Liberian girl
Dancer (black cat), singer (Bella Voce), artiste, Sailor, Sis

Always remember, never forget
You are a phenomenally phenomenal woman

I thank God for you every day
The answer to my prayers
My most beautiful creation
My bestie, I admire you

From your eclectic taste and your love of music
To your direct approach and sometimes brutal honesty
I'm still licking my wounds from when you made me throw
away prized possessions because I'm supposedly a hoarder
Yours is a beauty that radiates from within and shines
outwardly as a beautiful light
You are the manifestation of the very best

Always remember, never forget
You are a phenomenally phenomenal woman

Our mother-daughter bond
A love that cannot be broken by time, space, or distance
How can I describe a love so profound,
A love that makes my heart so full it could burst from its
depth and intensity?
It's like trying to describe the pleasure of the rays of the sun
on your skin
Just enough warmth, just enough light
To make you bask in the sheer joy of being in its presence
You bring joy like the joy that I feel when grey skies become
clear and I glimpse a rainbow
That is the joy that you bring

Always remember, never forget
You are a phenomenally phenomenal woman

With you, I can dance
With you, I can sing
I can laugh. I can cry. You bring balance.
You have been given the gifts of leadership, Strength, power,
integrity, and empathy

You are a

Jewel.

Attentive, assertive, articulate and accepting

Secure, satisfied, strong, and sensitive

Mentor and motivational

Intelligent and inspiring

Non-judgmental and you have

Endurance

Always remember, never forget.

You are a phenomenally phenomenal woman

We celebrate you

The Moles on My Left

I've always liked my moles
Especially the ones on my left
At the base of my toe
On the inside of my heel
At the top of my calf
On my pinky finger
Below my eye
On my collarbone
Points de beaute
That's how I want to be seen
Having left a beautifully unique mark on the canvas of your
life
A point de beaute that catches your eye and makes you smile
Present but not brash
Like a sprinkle of sparkle

Black and Sexy

Powerful

Luxurious

Strong

Dark as licorice

Charcoal

Blue-black

Midnight

Ebony

Onyx

Smooth against my skin

Tantalizing

Classic

Those moves

Hugging curves

Pulse racing

Pulse quickening

All eyes on me when I'm with you

I can't wait to experience your roar

As we shift

Slow then fast

Giving me the ride of my life
I love you
Don't they know who you are
Black and sexy?

You're my ...

Caramel Delight

Tall caramel deliciousness

Soul-stirring eyes

Lips that seduce

Words that caress

Stimulating my mind with your intellect

Awakening

That smooth, suave crimson and cream

I see you

Strong, father, son, brother

I see you

I see your knowledge
The answers within the reach of your fingertips
Research like second nature
Intelligence

I see you
Protector
Man of strength, faith, prayer, humility
Leader
Intellectual
Eclectic taste

I see you
Harmonious melange of gentleness, strength, humor,
disciple, and cultures
Exploration

I see you
I'd like to get to know you

If I could weave the words of a song
This is what I'd say
Power
Golden

You're my "Brown Sugar Babe

I get high off your love"

"How did you find your way back in my life?"

Queue "Dance me to the end of love"

Tu me fais entendre une nouvelle chanson

Celle de la joie

The voodoo that you do so well me fait frissoner

Le gout sucre de tes levres

"Just like candy – Chocolate, Vanilla, Strawberry"

Strawberry banana Kerns

Rich

Intoxicating

Charming, clever congenial

Kaptivating

My Sorors

All my life, I wanted a sister

Someone who got me – who understood me

Someone who was my companion

Someone with whom I shared the comfort of familiarity

Spelman

Sisterhood

Divas (Diverse Innovative Vivacious and Alluring)

The essence of a Spelman woman

United

Who are those girls –

Those Deltas?

"You got to work and pray and have the GPA to be a Delta"

Rush

Chapter President – high school valedictorian

So was I.

I want this sisterhood

Those Deltas

Standing out

Show deference and be ready to pledge in the South

Not yet

Search and find
Search and find
Search and find

Then it happened
Divine connections

The sisterhood before the sisterhood
Gracious
Helpful
Encouraging
Selfless, not selfish
Discerning
Risk-taker (because you always take a risk when writing a letter)
See and nourish the potential
Leader
Articulate
Empowered
Educated
Beautiful

Crossing those burning sands

Tears of joy

Fullness

Melodious voices

Oath

Sisterhood

Leadership

You can do it

I will help you

Where are you? I didn't see you at chapter meeting

You can call on me

I got you

Never alone

That's my LS, I got to get off the phone

Let's roll

Be OWT

Outstretched arms

Sisterhood

Challenge

Encourage

Advocate

Research

Be on time

You can do it

Cat raggedy

Excuses

Excuses are monuments

Get ready and stay ready

My mother was a Delta, I've been a Delta for 50 years

Stand up, speak out

If you are wrong, be wrong with confidence

Never alone

I will always have a sister

First 19,

Then sisters across the globe

That's my front

That's my back

Quad of the line

Brick house

Tuck that pinkie in

Let me fix your hair

Everyone, suck in your stomachs

My thighs are throbbing

Take the picture, pleeease

Hold it, hold it

Sweetheart song

Through dating, marriage,
birth, divorce, graduation,
death
Life's highs and lows

Never alone
My Sorors
Sophisticated
Dynamic
Phenomenal
Courageous
Effortless
Compelling
Invigorating

Loyal
Compassionate
Determined
Dedicated
Honest
Loving
Hopeful
Community conscientious
Accomplished
Go-getters

Ambitious

Sisterly

You have unwavering faith. You DO Service

You show AGAPE love and PROPINQUITY

My Sorors

Beloved Dears, Delightful Dolls, and Divastating Divas

Our color: red

The color of boldness

We are captivating

Powerful

A forever bond

AOML

Soror Estella Wells

San Bernardino Riverside Area Alumnae Chapter

Spring 2014

Who He Is, His Cane, His Colors

Crimson blazer-wearing leaders.
Men of authority and distinction
Those karasmatic and kaptivating men of
Kappa Alpha Psi

Tapping that cane – throwing it high
The step or shimmy that catches her eye
Those dapper and distinguished men of Phi Nu Pi

You are Debonair, Cravat-wearing
Men of Achievement
God-fearing, Persistent, Diligent, Intelligent, Hardworking,
Ethical
Determined. Committed, Gentleman who have love for
community

Who He Is, His Cane, His Colors

Your cane
It upholds. It provides support. It brings strength.
Tossed in the air. Exchanged with another.
In your hands, its tapping becomes the rhythm of
celebration.

The naked eye sees a cane – hand gripping its curved handle.
The transcendental eye can see that cane flipped around.
Used to lift up. Used to uplift.

Who He Is, His Cane, His Colors

Could it be, that kream interlaced with ribbons of krimson
Mimics the way that you are emphatically interconnected
With your brothers? With your community?

That krimson and kream. The colors of that cane
Like blood vessels woven between bone and muscle
What are you without your brother?
What are we without you?

To your Silhouettes, you are
Orderly, Original, Debonair, Honorable, Responsible,
Dutiful, Educated,
Caring, Committed to the Bond, and Confident.

Your sisters see you
Training our young men. Standing in the gap. Seeing the
need. Imparting wisdom.
Paying it forward. Wise Village Elders
Iron sharpening that which is not yet iron.
We see you.

To your mentees, you are Intelligent, Caring,
Open-minded, and Kind

Who He Is, His Cane, His Colors

Noble, needed, noetic
Ubiquitous influence
Prestigious and patient
Eclectic, efficacious

Keen, knowledgeable, kind
Accomplished
Powerful
Passionate, poised
Astute

By either name, you are extraordinary

Beautiful Felicia

Two words to describe you are Radiant and Fierce.

Radiant because you walk with confidence and authority.

You bring light and enlightenment.

You have a warmth that draws others to you.

Fierce

From the Latin ferus, meaning "untamed."

In French, fiers means "fierce, brave, proud."

The Urban Dictionary defines fierce as the combination of a positive mental spirit, bold words, and unapologetic actions used collectively.

Fierce

You are fueled by your faith and your convictions.

Like habaneros, you are bold and spicy.

You describe habaneros as flavorful and delicioso and fiery.

You, too, bring fire, energy, boldness, and zest to your village.

Positivity
With your daily devotionals, inspirational cards, and
thought-provoking whiteboard quotes, you inspire.
Please don't try to put her in a box.
She's far too complex
You are a blend of hip-hop, neo-soul, and classical
ingredients.
Princesses Nubiennes: "Makeda etait reine belle et
puissante."
Mixed with a little James Brown: "Say It Loud, I'm Black and
I'm Proud."
You can throw many signs: fist raised high, West side, DST
pyramid.

Please don't try to put her in a box.
She's far too complex
Don't you know?

She's a little Maya Angelou
It's the fire in her eyes,
And the flash of her teeth,
The swing in her waist,
And the joy in her feet.
She's a woman
Phenomenally. Phenomenal woman.

That's her.

She's a little Nikki Giovanni:
"She was born in the Congo. She walked to the Fertile
Crescent and built the Sphinx ... She's so hip, even her errors
are correct ... So perfect, so divine, so ethereal, so surreal, she
cannot be comprehended except by her permission"
A little Sojourner,
Leaving no man behind but with a 21st-century twist:
Leading the disenfranchised to economic self-sufficiency
through affordable housing development
Influenced by a little astrology (Sagittarius), Deepak Chopra,
and a little Pastor Diego
Please don't try to put her in a box.
She's far too complex

Groomed for greatness
Anointed and prayed over every morning
Homework: reading and writing assignments
USC, Berkeley, Abundant Living, Toastmaster
Extraordinaire, Diversity and Inclusion Advocate, MBA,
Theologian, Real Estate Broker. Entrepreneur
You're bustin' at the seams with knowledge and expertise
Please don't try to put her in a box.
She's far too complex

Though the pace may be chaotic and frantic, she stands tall.
She can,
Because she's got theme songs to keep her charged.

The Testimony
"But my relationship too strong for real I'm a saint. A child of
God and if you hate me then you ain't
Be the only G I know to take it all with no triggers
So I put my faith in Him and never no n...
As a result of that I'm cool, seem like I'm never nervous"
"I got the V.I.C.T.O.R.Y
I got no reason to fear, I got Jesus on my side, I got that aaaaa
Vs Up"
"Won't he do it!
Won't he do it
Willhe wonthe wonthewillhe wont he do it!"

The light of her eye, Princess Naomi awaits:
"How did you know? Did God tell you?"
You are beautiful Naomi. "I know, Mama."
In the same way that you compliment her,
It is my privilege to do the same for you
"You is kind, you is important, you is..."
You are Beautiful! And you are so much more!

You are a Boss: visualizing success and taking action (Vision Board and Passion Planner Queen)

You are a Diva: Diverse, Innovative, Vivacious, Virtuous, Alluring, and Anointed

Favored, focused, and fabulous
Encouraging, exceptional, effervescent, epicurean connoisseur, and equipped
Loving, loyal, and a leader
Intelligent and inspirational
Caring, cultured, courteous, and compassionate
Independent
Accomplished and awesome

We are graced by your unadulterated, powerful presence.

Princess

Regal, Authority, Leader
Elegance in Motion, Cultured
Refined, Gentile, Bourgeois
Resilient, Go-getter

A woman of God
Prayer warrior
True friend and sister
Virtuous vessel

With a dash of je ne sais quoi

"Ciao" when she gets off the phone or

I love you, Soror!

Elegant, fashionista, and beautiful

She embodies Savoir faire

Equally elegant wearing her beret

with a Parisian Flair

Her DST brimmed hat

Her fascinator for church or chapter meeting

Or wide-brimmed sun hat

She can give elegance lessons to Coco Chanel, June Ambrose

Auburn-colored locks

Fiery and fierce

She's the sister who forces you to level up

In a truly loving way or if you need her to keep it real

She can go there, too

You know she's from Chicago

She's a Delta: Dynamic, Empowered Leader Accomplished

Bling,

Mu Chi Charter member

Advisor of the Year

SBRAAC Past President

Our Soror/Spec

Perseverance, passionate, trustworthy, a friend, a sister,
loving, caring, always available
Keep it real
Bring the Chicago out
You can't do it all. You have to pick and choose
They better recognize I'm your spec and we don't roll like
that
Sensitive, tender-hearted
But don't let the petite size fool you

No need to read a Ritual
She is a living example of
compassion, courtesy, dedication, fellowship, fidelity,
honesty, justice, purity, and temperance.
No doubt you are entering the home of a Delta
From the foyer
Stairway landing
From the elephant paper towel holder
To the red tp
She's the Soror who will fix your hair, arrange your necklace,
tell you to get that report in, tell you to take a vacation, help
you arrange the vacation and enjoy the vacation with you,
and has the pictures to prove it

She is known for many colloquialisms
Drop it like it's hot
Get ready and stay ready
Let's roll! Let's do this
"Fried chicken is good. God is better than that!"
Be on point!

Talented, World Traveler, Great Organizer
Model – that classic turn
You got to stop, pause, admire, and love her
Iron that sharpens iron.
Genuine and Loving
Elegant, Caring, Sisterly, Sophisticated
Faithful and True Friend, Caregiver,
Intelligent, Independent, Cultured,
Confident
and a sister in whom I confide
No judgment...

Protective, Passionate,
Fashionista, Quintessential Entrepreneur
She's a **Boss**

Laughter, Dance, Libations, Food, Home
Beautiful, Tenacious, Head Held High

Fortitude

Choreographer, Concierge

Elegance in Motion.

Dedicated and

never backs down from challenges.

If there is a will, there is a way by God's grace.

Priceless, powerful, poised

Regal

Intelligent, innovative

Noble

Cultured, caring, confident, counselor, compassionate

Eloquent, encouraging, energetic

Sweet and sassy

Sophisticated

De mon part et de la part de mon 3eme

Du font de nos coeurs on te remercie enormement pour ton

amour et

pour tes conseils

Il ne fallait jamais frapper 3 fois

T'as tojours etait la pour nous

Notre chere Spec

AOML

Jazz

Jazz is like food to my soul
It calms me
Smooth
Gliding
Warmth enveloping me
Putting me at ease
Brings a smile to my face
Relaxes me

The beat
Slow enough to not make my skin glisten
Fast enough to make me tap my feet
Like that steady, rhythmic beat of the metronome
Balance. Warm
Easy

The rhythm
At times upbeat
Pace that quickens, but then...
It always settles

Cool jazz
Slow and easy
The kind of sound that makes you say,
"Oh yeah, That's my song! That's my jam!"
The kind of rhythm that makes you want to slow dance

Smooth jazz
Draws you close like a dance partner
Close enough to feel their breath on your neck and their
heartbeat next to yours
Stepping together. Moving as one

Can you hear it? Can you hear that saxophone?
Can you hear Will's baritone voice?
Do you hear it?
Stella By Starlight
A song just for me
Jazz is like food to my soul

Poetess and Free Spirit

I never got her name
The fiery redhead from Minneapolis.
Fiberoptic Techie
Hippie who talked of her Castilian lover,
Travels to Spain and New Orleans

She had been an interpreter (my high school and college
dream job)
What do you think of what's going on?
Gen X?
Millennials?
Politics?
Coronavirus?

We talked of our mutual love of writing and poetry.
Who shall I look for you as?
How do you get published?
The art of being able to translate sentiment into words
Who's your favorite poet?

Free Spirit spoke of her recent Norwegian cruise
Where there were jazz and debauchery (her words, not
mine).
As an artist, I appreciate her choice of words
As a woman, I appreciate the reckless abandon with which
she lives

I think of my Aunt Jo.
That hippie connection.
Whether they might have been kindred spirits.
Are all hippies created equal?

Free Spirit talked of her favorite author
And left me with the beautiful poem caminando

The Poetess and Free Spirit
May our paths cross again

Coleman Love

A brother-sister bond like no other
History
Brother Frank Coleman and Soror Edna Brown
Howard University
Two people of similar educational and ethical backgrounds
Trail Blazers
Founding members of the two most dynamic organizations,
Brother Frank Coleman and Soror Edna Brown
Unequivocally leaders of leaders.
Omega Psi Phi united with Delta Sigma Theta
Community service,
Empowerment,
Sisterhood and brotherhood

Coleman Love

A multitiered and multifaceted love.
It can be an expression of
Eros — Romantic Love. ...
Pragma — Enduring Love. ...
Ludus — Playful Love. ...

Philia — Affectionate Love. ...
Storge — Familiar Love. ...

But now that I've given you a little history, let me get down
to the crux.
Allow me to get to the juicy part –
The Coleman Love relationship between Priceless Ro and
Bernard

Your Coleman Love
A bond with such depth that
It mirrors the interconnectedness of Adam and Eve

From her creation, Eve was interconnected from within
An already fully formed and integrated part of Adam –
Even before she was removed from his side
Eve was drawn out to accompany Adam
So that they might walk side by side

Your Coleman Love
Like Adam and Eve
The foundation of your partnership was perfectly and
divinely designed
A part of one another even before you met
Like yin and yang, you complement each other

A bond between two who are equally yoked

Your Coleman Love soundtrack
Is a little "Atomic Dog" mixed with a little "To Be Real"
A little "Drunk In Love" with a little "Found"
He'd say, "So glad I found you!"
She'd say, "She ain't looking for another,
He's got everything she wants and needs"
He would sing "You're The Best Part"

When a man truly loves a woman, she becomes his
weakness.
When a woman truly loves a man,
He becomes her strength.
This is called exchange of power
Your love through the seasons
Purple: Regal
Gold: Powerful
Crimson: Bold
Cream: Pure

An Omega Man
He's a man for whom
Manhood, Scholarship, and Perseverance are essential
He is a leader

He is a mentor

An Omega Man is someone passionate about family and work,

He is confident and truthful

He has integrity

He is a scholarly gentleman of action

A Delta woman

A woman of Faith

Accomplished and Ambitious

Dynamic, Determined, and Dedicated

Loyal, Loving, and Honest

Sophisticated and Sisterly

Compelling and Community Conscientious

She's a Diva: Diverse Innovative Vivacious/Virtuous,

Alluring and Anointed

A Phenomenally Phenomenal woman

An Omega man + a Delta woman

Now that's a dynamic duo

Together They Are

Courageous, compassionate conquerors

Loyal

Original, obsequious, opulent

Omega, optimistic overcomers

Loyal leaders

Valiant victors

Endearing, equipped, and enlightened

Exceptional

Motivated mentors ministering through service

Anointed, accomplished, achievers

Noble, noetic

Birthday Blessings

Diva

Beautiful

Classy

Committed

Disciplined

Educator

Focused and fabulous friend

Mentor

Sister

Songstress

Chicago

Like the city from whence she hails

She's got that Chi-town Cosmopolitan air

Perhaps because of her urban-chic style and renaissance taste

Whatever it is

She's got savoir-faire

She's a sophisticated, goal-oriented woman of action

A go-getter

Music lover of eclectic taste
From House to Gospel and R&B
From Jazz to Funk and Pop

"Sorry you can't define her
Sorry she breaks the mold
Sorry she speaks her mind
Sorry she don't do what she's told
Sorry if she don't fake it
Sorry if she comes too real
She can never hide what she really feels"

She's real.
Sometimes raw
Sometimes fiery
ALWAYS passionate

The consummate professional
She can multitask like no other
Hold a teleconference, take notes, and text simultaneously –
you know you seen her do it
She wears that invisible "S" across her chest
Liaison extraordinaire is her superpower –
Able to effortlessly initiate and maintain lasting connections
in a single bound

Superpowers 2 and 3 impacting the community and making sure you are photo-ready – visibility, right angle, and lighting

God. Goals. Grind.
Queen
Boss

She's an artist's Muse
D'Angelo would say, "Skin is caramel with the cocoa eyes"
Eric Roberson would say she's "Picture Perfect"
She grooves to Teri Hunters' rhythmic beat and the lyrical notes of "Wonderful"
Charles Bibbs captured her beautiful flowing locks in "Adorning Glory"

P is for purpose
I is for imaginative
P is for passionate
E is for energetic
S is for sophisticated

Compassionate, caring, and charismatic

Helpful

Empowered and exceptional educator

Resilient, resourceful, and reliable

Young, for you are only as old as the woman you feel

Loyal leader

There Goes My Baby

HBCU College Fair

Excitement

Who did you see? Was it Grambling?

No, Alabama A&M

My heart leaps

Memories of The Classic

A&M vs State

Battle of the Bands

He doesn't know about that

He DOES know that the Bruhz stepped

And that leaves a marked impression

Men of Omega Psi Phi stepping

The rhythm, the strength, the agility, and the presence

He throws up the hooks and I laugh

Of course, I run to tell my LS – temporarily distracted by

possibilities of a mother-son Coleman Love

Can I go tonight?

The dynamic of the dialogue changes all too quickly for me

The talk between child and parent shifts to the discourse

between a young man and a woman

A man and a woman

"You keep trying to hold on, Mom. Let me be a man!"

My heart is both crushed and full at the same time

He has become a man

So quickly

He's just my baby boy who somehow towers over me

How do I help him become a man?

This is what I have been trying to do –

Surrounding him with positive male role models

So many lessons still to be taught

The urgency is now intensified

It's coming quicker and quicker

The intensity becoming stronger and stronger

How to budget

How to navigate transportation – How to figure out how to
get home

How to cook

Who will watch over him?

"Mom, the idea of leaving you seems weird. What if
something happens when I'm gone?

What if something happens to Dad, or you, or Nathaniel?"

"Nothing will happen.

You've got to live your life now, son, like your sister."

How do you reassure yet equip your child for possibilities?
Lord, give me strength and guidance
Help me let go of the baby whom I held in my arms
Whom I smothered with kisses
Help me to respect him as a man
Show me how to help him spread his wings

My heart breaks
But I am so happy
Happy knowing that God has given him favor
Huge doors of opportunity are on his path
Opportunities so great, we cannot yet even intellectually
grasp
Overflowing favor awaits him

There goes my baby

Mon Cher Sunu Gaal

Neither time, nor space, nor langue vivante (or how much
French or Wolof I may or may not remember).
Nothing can separate me from mon cher Sunu Gaal

Cinq
The number of years I spent immersing myself in its intricate
culture
My love grew so deeply,
The experiences resonated so profoundly,
That almost 40 years later
I am still awakened by dreams of being in my old
neighborhood
Il y a un lien si fort que malgre le temps et la distance,
je ressens deep in my spirit quand ma tata n'est pas en bonne
santee ou qu'une niece s'est mariee ou
qu'elle viens d'accoucher
I still yearn to revisit mon coin

Tastes of la jeunesse
Des maades (sucrees ou avec du sel et du piment)

Pain thon but not the sophisticated kind. The kind sold from
an aluminum yellow stand
served by a man who had no worries about food inspector
visits or obtaining permits.
I can almost taste the sweet deliciousness of fresh mangos
secretly plucked from my neighbor's tree.
Made-to-order beignets ou pastec shared with friends.
Des lentils made by my bestie
My reward for successfully having made my way past
ferocious Bien Sage
Ceeb u jeen ou poulet yassa – au bol bien sur
The sweet taste of bissap
Who would have thought that there would be days when I
would gladly suck on the corner of a plastic bag to be
rewarded by le jus de bouile (made from pain de singe)
frozen treat
Awakened by the aroma of fresh bread floating through my
window at daybreak
Treats of des nems when my grades were good
Du laax, Gertees toubab,
Pain de singes – all became familiar tastes
Les 3 vers de the also known as athaya. Something so sweet
that you don't mind the burned tongue!

Places

Marche Sandaga

Frighting yet exciting

The shopaholic in me loved the merchandise everywhere

I have never liked to barter, nor do I like large crowds, but I
frequently found myself drawn to its door

Travel

Il n'y a rien come un Sotrac plein de gens

Pressed so close together, you can almost feel your
neighbor's breath on your neck.

Maximum capacity?

It ain't full until someone is practically screaming that a limb
is stuck in the closing door

Des Car Rapids with no seatbelts

Hot, hot sand beneath my feet

Walking delicately so as not to arrive with totally dusty
shoes and ankles

Le Quartier

Les bonnes qui ballaient les cours tot le matin avant que la
famille se leve

School rivalries between Lycée Kennedy and Notre Dame

Between Lycée D'Application and Blaise Diagne

Rivalries between Sacre Coeur and Cathedral were set aside
as we prepped for great equalizers:
Le DFEM et le Bac
OMG the stress of the studies
But the fun

L'Amitie
Pass the drink and pass the food
No hand sanitizer
Drinking straight from your friends' drink bottles
No thought of American cooties
Oh, the fun that we had at Amitie 2
Les Bocandes, les Strauss, les Correia, les Ndoyes and les
Dioufs. Les Trusts
Evenings in front of someone's house
Dancing in the streets
Waiting for Ton Ton to get home smartly dressed in his
uniform and Tata qui descendait du travail habillee en robe
de sage femme
Lively games of Monopoly
Borrowed engine de notre voisin

La Musique
What is life without music
Sabina

T'es ok

Immigres

Michael Jackson

And still the melody continues as my subconscious recalls

Expressions

Ndank ndank moy jaap golo ci ni

Dafa saaf det

Xale bu reo

Ndeye saan

Li li la li

Ciim

Right hand wringing with snapping sound used when it's

too hot or too hard

Shoo too too

Sucking of teeth that survived the transatlantic voyage

because African Americans still do it

Nangafef

Or how I was teased by my 4eme MIC classmates

Danfaduf instead ... to see if I caught the difference

La Politesse

Tout le monde se leve quand le prof rentre dans la salle

If faut serrer la main de tous

Deux ou trois bises (a teenager taking full advantage of the opportunity to kiss the cute boys or vice versa)

La Dance
Meringue
Secousees
Ventilator
Breakdancing (Bougie Bb qui a fait des cours de brkdance a l'Universite)
Bruno who somehow managed to get on TV dancing the meringue
Loud parties. I could hear the music but MY Daddy wouldn't let me go – strategically placed himself in the living room so he could see every time I left my bedroom and I didn't hit that back door. Of course, I know why they never oiled the springs of the screen door.
It was so they could hear every time the door was opened.
The tactic worked pretty well until my senior year quand je suis tombee amoureuse de WS.
Neither time, nor space, nor langue vivante (or how much French or Wolof I may or may not remember).
Nothing can separate me from mon cher Sunu Gaal.

My 19

What is a torch?

It's not a candle

In darkness, it doesn't just light the way

It is a blazing beacon

It has an undeniable power, strength, and substance

My 19

My beautiful sisters

My sweet sisters

My tough sisters

My ride-or-die sisters

My prayer warrior sisters

My "Hook you up" sisters

My "Let's get it together" sisters

My "What's your work strategy?" sisters

My "Let me vent to you" sisters

My "Gurrl, did you hear?" sisters

My "Let's just analyze what happened at chapter/committee meetings" sisters

My "Stand up for yourself!

Believe in yourself!" sisters

My "I got you" sisters

Strive

Proud to be

Brickhouse

Sweetheart song

I really don't think they had a clue

When we were named The 19 torches of DSTinction

They had no clue about the powerhouses we were and are

Nurse, Doctor, Lawyer, Minister, Therapist, Analyst, Social Worker, Educator, Entertainment Manager, Student, Community Activist, Poet, Playwright, Entrepreneur

To each other, we are fashion consultants, on-call therapists, business consultants, educational consultants, parenting consultants, dating consultants

We are Second Vice Presidents, Presidents, Chairs, Co-Chairs, Directors.
We are Empire builders
My 19.
We're strong, compassionate, courageous Women of DSTinction
What echoes in my mind is
"let me be a torch down truth's dim..."

I really don't think they had a clue
when we were named The 19 torches of DSTinction

We've held each other up
Through sickness, births, marriages, deaths, divorces, graduations

Oh yeah, we have a bond
Though at times the cord may become frayed from friction.
Though the right end may not see the left
The bond is strong
The bond
Woven cords of faith,
Individual strands comprised of our varied and diverse experiences and strengths
The bond is strong and grows more precious with each passing year

I'm finally starting to spread my wings and become the
woman who I'm designed and destined to be
and I am sooo thankful for you
For your influence
I am thankful for a moment in time and moments in time
with you
You held my hand
You literally brought me food
Even when I wasn't being greedy like that key lime cake at
Dee's
but seriously, you fed me
With physical food
With spiritual food
With prayers
Pushing my back
Helping me stand up and stand straight

So many memories had and to be had
Sweating bullets at Kym's house trying to learn those
Founders
We've danced, cried, laughed, vacationed, worked, and
worshiped together

Rolling with my sissies

Listening to gospel or

"I don't f with you"

Watermeloning it through the Beta Hymn

I always wanted to own the song

all while knowing too well that my frame was not that of a

Brick House,

But ohhh, when it became my line song

I felt and will always feel it to the core!

We are

Talented and tenacious

Outstanding and overcomers

Resourceful and resilient

Courageous

Helpful

Exceptional

Sensational

Tomorrow Is Not Promised

If the family is divided, may we make efforts to reunite now,
for tomorrow is not promised
Let your light shine now, for tomorrow is not promised
Let go of the hurt, pain, and heartache, for tomorrow is not
promised
May my words uplift now, for tomorrow is not promised
May I cause you to laugh, sing, and be empowered now, for
tomorrow is not promised
May I think now of my legacy, for tomorrow is not promised
Let me be a torch now, for tomorrow is not promised
May I strive to reach my highest potential daily, for
tomorrow is not promised
May I leave a legacy like a mirror reflecting God's goodness,
compassion, and grace now,
For tomorrow is not promised
And when I go home to glory, may I have lived a life that
brought our community and family closer
For tomorrow is not promised

You Got Me

You got me floating on a cloud
So relaxed
Seeing your face
Feeling your arms around me

Simple pleasures
You rubbing my hand
Me rubbing yours
Riding in your car. Reading poetry to you
Vibing

You got me making mixtapes
Well, really, creating playlists in a Neosoul mood
"Share My Life" – Kem
"You're My Lady" – D'Angelo
"That Magic" – India Arie
"Say Yes" – Floetry

You got me Soso sososo sososo
I can barely even eat – And you know that's major
I just want to write…

About you.
To you

So relaxed. Still floating on a cloud
Simple pleasures
Just looking at you.
Caressing your cheek

Anticipation

You got me like a Gain commercial
Wanting to inhale you
Your essence

You got me feeling ... What's that word?
SuperCalafragilistic

The Rhythm of Your Metronome

The metronome measures the beat
From slow to fast.
It sets the pace
Much like how the heart sets the rhythm
It measures the beat and pace of your life
Your metronome measures the ebbs and flows
Your metronome beats:
Build. Support. Prepare. Serve.

Your journey, like the keys of a piano, is marked by sharps
and flats,
The keys of the piano. Your path from New York to
California to Mississippi
Your metronome beats –
Build. Support. Prepare. Serve.

Build

Davis Bacon.
Build musical creativity
Build: Airport.

Support

Caregiver to mother

Support as a grandfather

Support – because you are inherently generous

Prepare

From the Homeboy project to Hymtimacy to sulking and
ministry in Atlanta Hartsfield

Prepare

Birthed in Brooklyn, New York

Man inspired, influenced, and developed by your travels

Los Angeles Redlands Desert Hot Springs – Arroyo De Paz,
Atlanta, Sacramento,

Hey Nineteen Publishing

Serve

A Pianist

You skillfully master the keys of the piano

The artistry of taking a sound and giving it life

From an inanimate object, bringing forth sound that becomes
a voice

the voice of the piano ushers in the Holy Spirit

You are the pianist recognizing the sharps and flats and
making them a beautiful melody

Flats are the mountaintop experiences, the great loves of
your life: Shawn/Cameron/Vanessa/Justin/Amarah
Grandbabies: Jaden and Kay-son
Sharps are the valleys: Alzheimer's. Lawyers. Social Security

You are a **songwriter** who has the unique ability to blend
music and message
Giving life through music

The medley of life through song
You are an artist for whom the melody of the song is equally
important as its message
"Highest Praise," "Never Would Have Made It"
"That's What Friends Are For," "Won't He Do It,"
"Joy Inside My Tears," "Blessed."

Your journey marked by a passion for Music and Ministry
Your voice – an instrument of highest praise

The rhythm of your metronome
Build. Support. Prepare. Serve.
The beat to your drum

Valiant and Victorious
Intelligent Intercessor
Numinous and Noetic
Compassionate, Confident, Courageous,
Equipped, Effectual, and Exalted

When I Look at You I See

To the 2019-2020 Kappa League Class
To My Sons, My Nephews, My Young Village Warriors

When I look at you I see

Budding Intellectuals
Brilliant young men thirsty for knowledge
You are Intelligent. Articulate. Outspoken.
Confident. Talented. Leaders.

When I look at you I see

Overcomers
This year, you've faced challenges and adversity AND you
have come out on the other side
You may have bent, but you did not break
You might have been discouraged or felt defeated
Yet you not only survived,
You've thrived.
You finished the year with a double major: matriculating the
curriculum of
both Kappa League and EMBODI

Strong Young Black Men
We're proud of you.
You are your brothers' keeper
You are extraordinary.
Continue to set goals.
Give of your time and your talent.
Be active. Be cautious.
Be engaged. Stay inspired.

When I look at you

I see and speak life into you reaching your highest potential
Because you are

Kings	**L**eaders
Accomplished achievers	**E**quipped with endurance
Passionate and positioned	**A**dvocates who shall be abundantly blessed
Purposeful	**G**rounded, generous young gentlemen
Anointed, appointed	**U**nique AND
	Exceptional

The Best Is Yet to Come

(Kappa League Mom)

Lessons from Michelle

1. Live your life. Travel. Travel a lot. Go to the places you've always dreamed of visiting. We saw you traveling the world.
2. Stand your ground. Be sure-footed about what you will and will not accept.
3. Further your education. Don't sell yourself short. Get that diploma. *I keep a picture of you in your cap and gown so I stay inspired.*
4. Take good care of yourself. Beautiful hair, nails done, and matching lipstick. You took the time.
5. When life knocks you down, get back up. You are an example of resilience.
6. Be generous. Always remember to send a card or give support, no matter the distance.
7. Don't waste time. Seize the day.

I can hardly believe that you're not here. But I have so much peace that your days were spent living your life like it was golden.
Motivated and mentor
Intelligent and inspiring
Caring, classy, and cultured
Helpful
Ethical and efficacious
Loyal and loving
Leader
Empowered and encouraging

Mi Tia

February 15, 2020

Beautiful

Academic

Courageous

Colorblind (*because love knows no color*)

Community builder

Passionate

Playful

Scholar

Supportive

Dreadlocks

Purple hair

Davieree's daughter
Jo
Sister
Her heartbeats Shelley, Rahdi, Hailey

Detroit
Wayne State. Member of Delta Sigma Theta Sorority Inc.
Claremont. PhD
Santa Monica. Pepperdine
World traveler

Precious memories
Sock puppets
Reading stories
Her laugh
Dancing
Roller skating in River Rouge
Singing "I got shoes, you got shoes, all of God's children got
shoes, when I get to heaven gonna put on my shoes, gonna
walk all over God's heaven"

Style maven
Boutique shopper (that's code for those specialty bargain
stores that aren't quite consignment shops)
Uniquely adept at designing stunningly beautiful, eclectic,
and colorful garb

Papa
Intelligent. Involved. Calm
Papa: a special name given by granddaughter to
grandmother.
So intimate. So unique

"We were reading a book in her house and then I told her a
story that I made up. She said she wanted to write it down
into a book."

And that made me smile because I was so happy
Don't we all feel that way?
How I loved **Mi Tia**

My confidante. She was the one I called with the news of
Jasmine's pending arrival. *Too scared to call my own mother.*

She is the one who, when she found out that I wanted to be a
Delta, sent me her own pledge pin.
She is the one who shares my love of language and travel

Mi Tia

Free spirit

Going all the way to Guatemala to improve her language skills.

Why take the easy route? Like her, make your life an adventure!

Why be just American? Fall in love with an Irishman named Sean and seek dual citizenship.

We all loved her

We are all family

Chosen family

Kindred souls

We have more than a biological bond

We are bonded by faith

We are bonded by values, education, challenges, life experiences

We are bonded by the support that she gave to us – that we gave to her

Simplicity, Peace, Integrity, Community, Equality, and Stewardship (SPICES)

Warrior.

Gentle Spirit.

Ray of Light

She had Black Girl Magic.

In heaven now with Mother, Aunt Sis, Mr. Brown, Miss Marie, and Raymond

Joyful

Optimistic

Adventurous, academic, artistic

Noble

Nurturer

Sincere, strong

Inspirational, having integrity

Sympathetic

Tender teacher

Exuberant, eclectic, empathetic

Regal

Trustworthy and talented trailblazer

Intentional

Adored

Special thanks to family that allowed me to include their beautiful memories

Martin

The strength of a name
Martin Mwalimu Kwakou Isaac
A name that foretold the character and strength you would embody
Martin: After Dr. Martin Luther King Jr.
Upstanding man of integrity, a powerful leader.
Mwalimu: Teacher after President Mwalimu Julius Nyerere
Kwakou: Honoring the tradition of having a day name. Male born on Wednesday – an homage to his parents' travels.

Bold. Powerful.
Strong. Fierce.
Direct. Polite.
Well-mannered

Curly-haired boy jumping in doorways
Going to sleep wearing his tan combat boots
"Did you have a good sleep, Mwalimuuuu? Did you have a good sleep, Mwalimu?" his mother sang

A man of international intrigue
Studying abroad
Trilingual: English, French, Spanish
Intro to French in Senegal
Horseback riding in Cameroon

Petit frere clothed in black
His mother's handyman
Tech-savvy Dungeon Master with his dragon Lunch
Archer, mage, warrior/swordsman, hand-to-hand combat
Tough, baseball bat-toting warrior

Cirque du Soleil
Pyro technical fireworks, lighting, stage, production
Life is your stage

I dare say, he is a man who has always chosen his own path
Not one to be shackled by society's norms or traditions
How could he be? This little Black boy from Mississippi
No one can tell you how to live, whom to love, what to wear,
where to go
He has a fierceness underneath which a tender heart of a
protector is found

His first love (after his mother, of course) was Tini.
Ou est Tini? Qui t'a dit que tu pouvais laver Tini?!
Please don't touch or wash Tini or you shall suffer the wrath!
His next love – his Gold Wing Motorcycle! The catalyst for
"Oh Lord, please be with all the men in our family"

You have chosen your own path
You have always been and shall always be
Your own distinctly unique person –
Claremont College –
Indian Springs –
Camp Cosby
Cours prives de Mathes et d'Espagnol
Sipping wine in Paris paired with a baguette or perhaps with
cheese
Citizen of the world
From Mississippi to DC,

From Alabama to Senegal,
From Cameroon and California to France, then Las Vegas

Memories
Honey-baked ham – Grandma always made sure to take one
to Las Vegas
His first vehicle: a truck
Riding on the back of your motorcycle
Speaking to each other in Spanish at the grocery store (our
secret language in Alabama)
Going to the library with Mom and getting crates of books
A strong shoulder to lean on.

The way a person laughs says so much about them
Yours is a deep, booming, boisterous laugh
Such is your footprint on our lives –
You are a rich, deep, heartfelt, strong presence
You are upstanding
A proud man of integrity.

The Strength of a Name
Martin Mwalimu Kwakou Isaac

Mature, marvelous
Adventurous, attentive
Reliable, resourceful
Talented, tremendous ability
Intelligent, international
Noble

She's Not Just My Soror, She's My Sister

My Soror
Crossing those burning sands into Delta Sigma Theta land
made us Sorors
Our Oath
We work together, pray together, stroll together, and break
bread together

My Sister
Ours is an intentional bond
My sister goes to battle with me and for me
My sister not only sees the best in me

She encourages me to grow into being my best self
With my sister, I can be vulnerable
My sister celebrates my accomplishments
My sister is a helping hand.

My Sister
She knows me

If I don't come to the chapter meeting, she calls
"We missed you, Sis. Are you okay? What can I do?"
My sister lifts me up in prayer
For my sister, I will drop the call with someone else
Because my sister has my heart and I have hers

MTAAC making an impact
May your bond become so close
May your love for one another become so strong
That you experience an overflowing bond of sisterhood
May you be not just Sorors.
May you be Sisters.

Mighty, motivating	**S**ensitive, supportive
Tenacious	**I**ntercessor, inspirational
Accomplished	**S**olidarity
Astute	**T**enderhearted
Charismatic, compassionate	**E**ncouraging, empathetic
	Resilient, reliable

Dedicated to the Charter Members of the
Murrieta Temecula Alumnae Chapter

My Front

Community Activist

Debutante

Dancer

Care Giver

Selfie Queen

Singer

Traveler

God has a sense of humor

Placing Bennett Belle next to Spelmanite.

Sisters with a common love of community service

Sisters to Morehouse Brothers

Both with a long-awaited dream to be fulfilled
Front and Back
Sisters in faith
The quest for sisterhood
Tre and Quad
Endured Pursuit and DST Closure
Sorors of Delta Sigma Theta Sorority, Inc.

Bonded from the day when I knew that you couldn't carry
your bag
I got you, girl, and you got me
We've supported each other through many of life's
challenges and rewards
Harrowing experiences like a hot air balloon festival and
Crimson and Cream prep
Most joyous occasions: Saying Yes to the Dress and signing
day

We're both bilingual
I speak French and Spanish
She speaks two dialects – code-switching between Ebonics
and the Queen's English
She connects effortlessly with boys from the hood and
Congressmen
She speaks both of their languages fluently

She's a little bad and a little bougie
She can meet you at the club or in the board room
Taking a trip to Disney Land or meeting you at the NAACP
National Convention. Whatever your pleasure

She's a Legacy
Heir of the Rucker Hughes dynasty
Post office, streets, proclamations, resolutions
Citizen of the Year and other awards are her birthright

My Front always keeps it real
You will recognize her by "Yes Lawd!" "Whazup?"
"Okaaay" with tongue smack/click
"Knowhatimsayn" and "Wooptywop"
Or "Aaay"

She's a singer extraordinaire
Music lover of eclectic taste
She grooves to Hip Hop, R&B, Neosoul
24k Magic – Bruno Mars. Happy Feelings – Frankie Beverly
& Maze
Right Hand Drake. Alright Ledisi and AOML

My Front

Always smelling good with her signature fragrances, oils, and body spray

She's a great dancer

Choreographing strolls. Making my sons crack up because she can do their dances

My Front is gorgeous

Beautiful green eyes *because she eats vegetables*

Beautiful hair. Beautiful spirit.

Though she may not recognize it yet,

She is a BOSS

May this serve as a reminder that she is inherently a member of the talented tenth. She's the crème de la crème

She is a Queen.

She was raised as such and shall continue to be so.

In Deltaland, Thug Passion is sometimes tough

But I am privy to her softer side and she is privy to my visceral side

With this 3 and 4, the seemingly tough one can let down her guard and the sensitive one can drop explicatives with no judgment

My Front

She loves hard. She loves strong. She loves deep

Loves her hubby, Michael J

Loves her family

Loves her fur babies

Talented	DelTa
Equipped for success	No more Excuses
Luminous, loyal leader	AlL of My Love
Intelligent	BrIck House
Empathetic	To BE Real
Creative and compassionate	What a Sigma Can't
Eloquent and empowered	SwEetheart Song

Black Girl Magic

Focused and Fabulous

Eloquent

Distinctive

Cultured

Devoted

No one has our style

Beautifully coiffed hair in styles that only we can do justice

to

Vibrant

Shoe game poppin'

Dressed with our own uniquely elegant flair

Divas

Diverse Innovative Vivacious Alluring and
Diverse Inspiring Virtuous Anointed

We
Bring light, Give from our hearts, and Mentor the masses

Women of Faith
Daughters of the Most High God
We are Blessed, Grateful, and Magnificent

BOSS Ladies
Goal-oriented
Beauty combined with intellect
We are about business

Smile Sparkle Shine

Exuberant

Gifted

Kind

Proud

BGM

We represent

If no one else tells you this today,

know that you are a

Dedicated to My Beautiful BGM Sisters

Monique

Shaq

Rhonesia

Erica

Mes Soeurs

In the stillness of the morning
As I think of you

You are reminders of
Principles
Strength
Compassion
Generosity
Humility
Community-mindedness
Leadership
Wisdom
You are my reminders
That grace, fortitude, and strength are clothed in a voice both
quiet and boisterous.
My reminders of mes raciness.
Groundedness.

Mes Soeurs
Melanin poppin' DIVAS (as in Diverse, Innovative, Virtuous,
and Anointed)

We are bonded by Senegal, education, womanhood, motherhood

Mes soeurs

A continuous reminder of sisterhood and its many faces.

Victorious and vivacious	**F**avored and fabulous	**A**nointed
Empathetic	**L**oving, loyal, leader	**I**nspirational intercessor
Visionary full of vitality	**O**utstanding, optimistic, overcomer	**C**onfident and compassionate
Empowered	**R**egal and resilient	**H**umble and hardworking
Tender and tenacious	**E**mpathetic and empowered	**A**ccomplished
Talented	**N**onpareil and noetic	
Exceptional	**C**ompassionate	
	Exceptional	

Your Witness

Dedicated to the McPherson Family

Your witness is a living, breathing Bible to others
Your witness is your walk
It is the thing that may draw others to Christ – whether you
know it or not
Your witness is the behavior that can shine so brightly that
others can grasp hope in a hopeless situation
They see your strength
They see faith in action
They can believe that change is possible
They may be convicted just by your witness

Your witness exemplifies the Fruit of the Spirit
Love, Joy, Peace,
Patience, Kindness, Goodness, Faithfulness, Gentleness, Self-
control

Your witness, like a beacon, shows
What is upstanding
What is upright

Hospitality

Generosity

Femininity

Kindness

The pursuit of excellence

Service

Leadership

Like a ripple made by a small pebble on still waters
Your witness shall continue to have a resounding impact
Thirty years later, your witness still resonates

In times of sheltering in place
As I raise my children
And as I look at my own role
I think of you
I have precious reminders of
What to expect, what I should be, and
What I can be

Your Witness

Your witness is seen in, perhaps to you, the most mundane
activities
Yet, these are lessons I remember from having spent time
with you

Generosity

Going out to eat to celebrate Jonathan's graduation

Your father taking care of the bill and your mother buying me shoes

Public Speaking

Standing up and introducing myself to the congregation

Tender Care

Your father putting gas in your mother's car

Femininity, Self-Care, and Beauty

Trips downtown to pick up your mother's beautiful custom-made hats

Trips to the salon for manicures (Theons #5)

Prepare Delicious Meals

DELICIOUS meals cooked by your mom

Surround Yourself with the Word

TBN on the television

Embrace Your Gift

Keep up with those piano lessons

Reference

Caesar, D., and H.E.R. (2017). Best part [Song]. On *Freudian*. Golden Child.

Clinton, G. (1982). Atomic dog [Song]. On *Computer games.* Capitol Records.

D'Angelo (1995). Brown sugar [Song]. On *Brown sugar*. EMI.

Downing, W. (1995). Stella by starlight [Song]. On *Moods*. UMG Recordings.

Knowles, B., and Jay, Z. (2013). Drunk in love [Song]. On *Beyonce*. Columbia Records.

Lynn C. (1978). Got to be real [Song]. On *Cheryl Lynn*. Columbia Records.

Mai, E. (2016). Found [Song]. On *Change*. 10 Summers Records, LLC.

Peyroux, M. (2005). Dance me to the end of love [Song]. On *Careless love*. Columbia Records.